Hip Hip Hooray! 2

Authors

Beat Eisele

Catherine Yang Eisele

Rebecca York Hanlon

Stephen M. Hanlon

Barbara Hojel

Consultant

Mayumi Tabuchi

LONGMAN ON THE WEB

Longman.com offers online resources for teachers and students. Access our Companion Websites, our online catalog, and our local offices around the world.

Visit us at longman.com.

Longman

Hip Hip Hooray! 2

CONSULTING REVIEWERS

Gareth Dewar, Bahrain • **Maria Amélia Marcus de Oliveira,** Associação Alumni, São Paulo, Brazil • **Lidy Olea,** Colegio Pumahue, Santiago, Chile • **Martha Quijano Morales,** Universidad Javeriana, Santafé de Bogotá, Colombia • **Julio del Aguila,** Instituto Guatemalteco Americano, Guatemala City, Guatemala • **Laura de la Vega Orantes,** Colegio Suger Montano, Guatemala City, Guatemala • **Shawna Beji,** ECC, Osaka, Japan • **Patricia Ruiz,** Kinki University, Osaka, Japan • **Joohee Oh,** Samteo Culture Center, Kyunggi, Korea • **Monica Chaparra Esquivel,** Colegio Galileo Galilei, Mexico City, Mexico • **Isabel Cristina Trenti,** Instituto Avance, San Luis Potosí, Mexico • **Gloria de Ho,** Universidad de Panamá, Centro Cultural Chino, Panama City, Panama • **Maureen Orama Arzán,** Nueva Escuela Montessori, Río Piedras, Puerto Rico • **Chen Huiwen,** Taipei, Taiwan • **Jayne Liu, Isabel Cheng,** KOJEN English Language School, Taipei, Taiwan • **Carmen de Guynn,** Colegio Bellas Artes, Maracaibo, Venezuela

Illustration credits
Storyline: Sheila Bailey
Practice pages: Olivia Cole
Gameboards: Adam Gordon

Photo Credits
Studio photos by Richard and Amy Hutchings

Page 35 sandwich, Peter Johansky/Index Stock Imagery; zoo, James Lemass/Index Stock Imagery/PictureQuest; **87** quilt, Phyllis Picardi/Index Stock

All other photos Artville, Corbis Royalty Free, Corel, EyeWire, PhotoDisc and PictureQuest.

Pearson Education, 10 Bank Street, White Plains, NY 10606

Vice president, director of publishing: Allen Ascher
Editorial director: Anne Stribling
Development director: Penny Laporte
Senior project development editor: Lucille M. Kennedy
Senior development editors: Barbara Barysh, Yoko Mia Hirano
Market research director: Louise Jennewine
Vice president, director of design and production: Rhea Banker
Executive managing editor: Linda Moser
Production manager: Liza Pleva
Associate managing editor: Sandra Pike
Director of manufacturing: Patrice Fraccio
Senior manufacturing buyer: Edie Pullman
Design and production: Bill Smith Studio
Cover design: Bill Smith Studio
Text font: Futura, modified

ISBN: 0-13-061202-2

Printed in the United States of America
14 15 16–RRD–12 11 10 09 08

Contents

Welcome!

Hello

How old are you?

I'm seven years old.

Where do you live?

I live in New York.

Your Turn

Classroom Objects

What's this?

It's **a pen**.

Your Turn

1. a book

2. a chair

3. a bag

4. a desk

5. a pencil

6. a ruler

Your Turn

1. pens

2. rulers

3. chairs

4. bags

5. tables

6. pencils

More Objects

Is this **a ruler**?

Yes, it is.

Is this **a bag**?

No, it isn't.

Your Turn

1. a ball

2. a cup

3. a bat

4. a cap

5. a pot

6. a gift

Colors

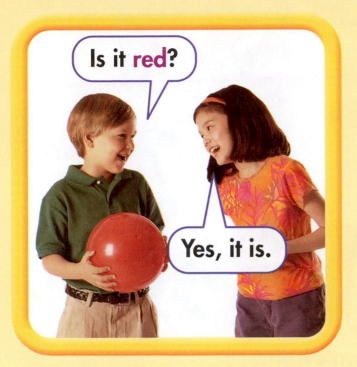

Your Turn

1. red

2. green

3. yellow

4. blue

5. brown

6. orange

7. black

8. white

What does he want?

He wants **fish**.

What does she want?

She wants **fruit**.

Your Turn

1. pizza

2. bread

3. noodles

4. milk

5. juice

6. water

Hip Hip Hooray!

Let's go help.

Okay. Let's make shoes.

Who is he?

He's a shoemaker.

Your Turn

She's a doctor.

He's a police officer.

He's a farmer.

She's a teacher.

He's a student.

Who is he?
He's a shoemaker.
He's a shoemaker.
Who is she?
She's a shoemaker, too.

Who is she?
She's a doctor.
She's a doctor.
Who is he?
He's a doctor, too.

Learn!

Who are they?
They're _____.

they're = they are

Listen and say.

Who are they?

They're **students**.

Your Turn

1. students

2. doctors

3. farmers

4. police officers

5. teachers

6. shoemakers

🎧 **Listen and say. Write.**

Who is he?

He's a student.

Who is she?

She's a student.

police officer
farmer

Write.

1. Who is she?

_____

She's a _____.

2. Who is he?

_____

He's a _____.

🎧 **Listen and say. Write.**

| teachers | farmers |
| students | doctors |

1. Who are they?

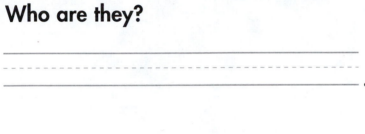

They're teachers .

2. Who are they?

_____
- - - - - - - - - - - -
_____ .

3. Who are they?

_____
- - - - - - - - - - - -
_____ .

4. Who are they?

_____
- - - - - - - - - - - -
_____ .

Talk About the Workshop!

Listen and say.

What are those?

They're **hammers**.

Your Turn

1. hammers

2. mops

3. shoes

4. rulers

5. pencils

6. nails

Learn About Sounds!

Listen and say.

mop

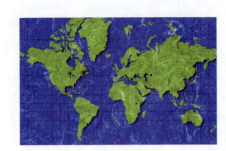
map

marker

nest

nail

nose

a b c d e f g h i j k l **m** **n** o p q r s t u v w x y z

Listen and touch.

m   n

Listen. Point and say.

Practice

🎧 Listen and say. Match.

1.

2.

3.

4.

5.

6.

m

n

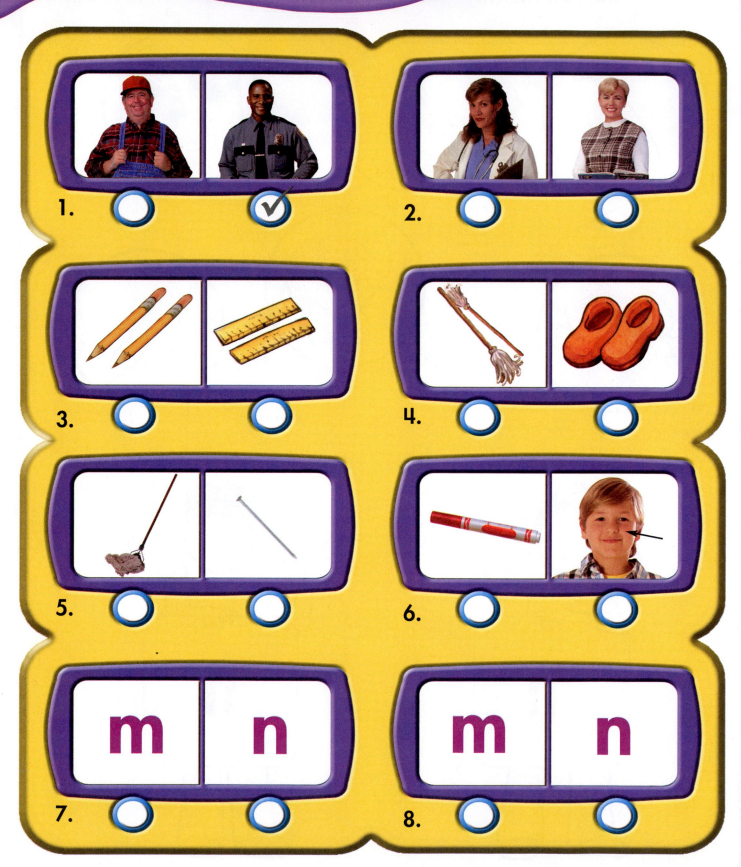

1.

2.

3.

4.

5.

6.

7. m n

8. m n

The Elves Help

Let's hurry!
Let's get busy!
Where's the pencil?
It's on the table.

Let's hurry!
Let's get busy!
Where's the ruler?
It's next to the cup.

Learn!

Listen and say.

Where are the shoes?

They're under the table.

Your Turn

Where are the hammers?

1. under

2. on

3. next to

Where are the rulers?

4. in

5. behind

6. in front of

Grammar **17**

Practice

🎧 Listen and say. Write.

Where is the book?

It's on the chair.

🎧 Listen and circle.

18 ✏️

Practice

> on   next to
> in   under
> in front of

1. **Where are the rulers?**

   _____

   They're _____on_____ the table.

2. **Where are the books?**

   _____

   They're _____ the bag.

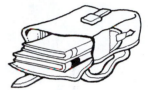

3. **Where are the students?**

   _____

   They're _____ the desks.

4. **Where are the cups?**

   _____

   They're _____ the milk.

5. **Where are the shoes?**

   _____

   They're _____ the bed.

✏️ 19

Talk About a Room!

Listen and say.

Where's the pencil?

It's next to the bed.

Your Turn

1. the bed

2. the lamp

3. the rug

4. the chair

5. the window

6. the door

Learn About Sounds!

Listen and say.

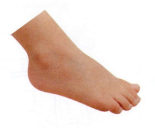

foot

fan

fish

vest

violin

van

a b c d e **f** g h i j k l m n o p q r s t u **v** w x y z

Listen and touch.

f   v

🎧 **Listen and circle. Write.**

Where's the pencil?

1. It's under the lamp.

2. It's under the bed.

3. It's under the rug.

4. It's under the window.

5. It's under the chair.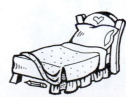

Practice

Listen and say. Match.

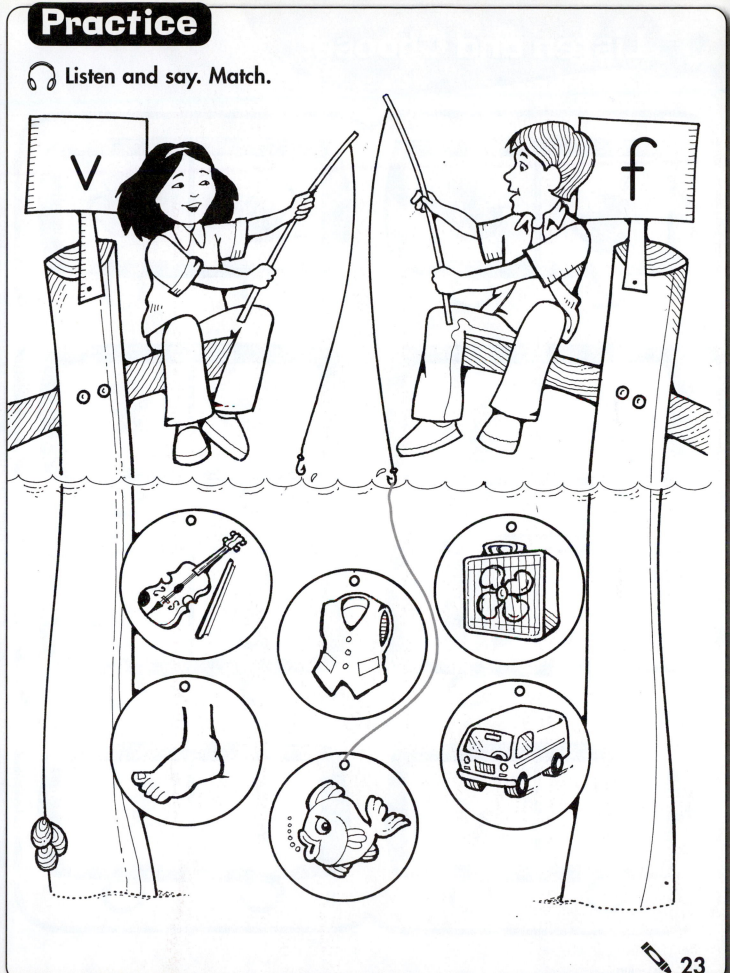

1.

2.

3.

4.

5.

6.

7. f v

8. f v

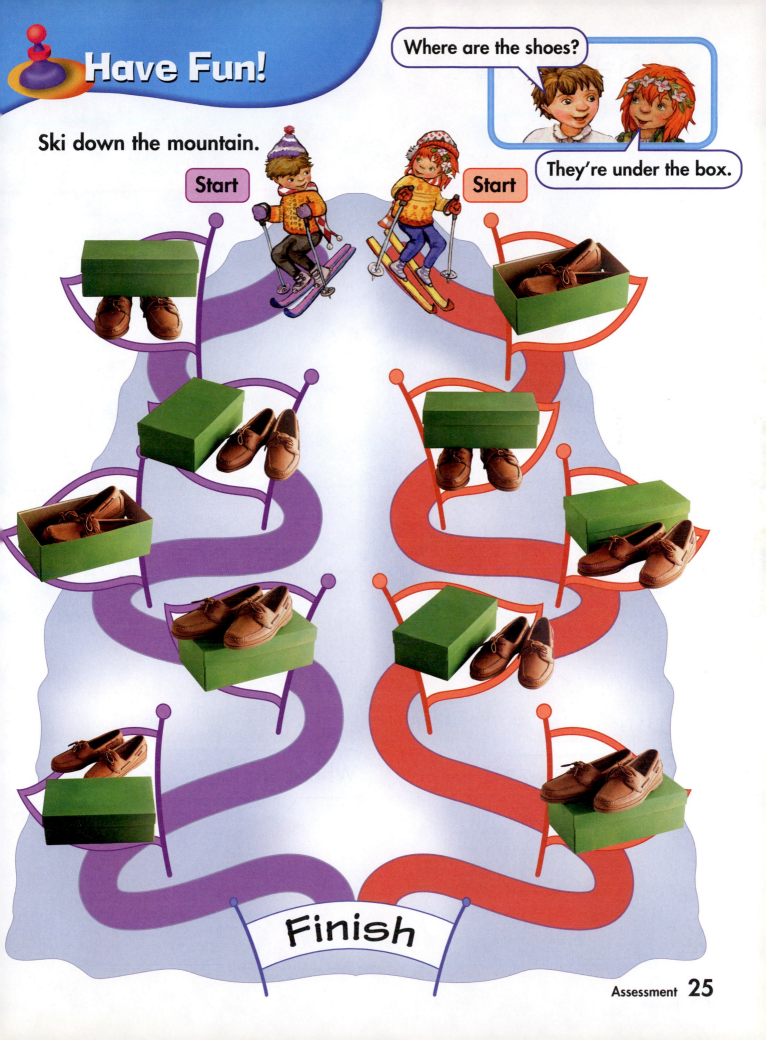

Listen and find.

Your Turn — Point and say.

What are those?

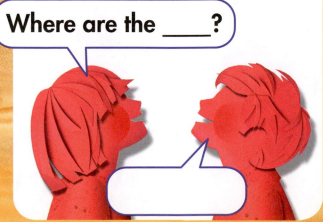

Where are the ____?

Role-Play Storytime (Units 1 and 2)

Who is he?

Let's hurry!
Where's the pencil?

Listen and say.

Can you **dance**?

Yes, I can.

I can dance.
I can whistle.
And I can make beautiful shoes!

Your Turn

hop

jump

walk

run

Look at me!
I can dance.
Can you dance, too?

Yes, I can.
I can dance.
I can dance, too.

Look at me!
I can whistle.
Can you whistle, too?

Yes, I can.
I can whistle.
I can whistle, too.

Learn!

Listen and say.

Can he _____?
Yes, he can.
No, he can't.
Can she _____?
Yes, she can.
No, she can't.

Can she hop?

Can he hop?

Yes, she can.

No, he can't.

Your Turn

Can she _____?

1. hop

2. walk

3. dance

Can he _____?

4. jump

5. run

6. whistle

Practice

🎧 **Listen and say. Write.**

Can you hop?

Yes, I can.

dance	jump
hop	walk
whistle	run

Write and draw.

I can _____.

Listen and say. Write.

1. Can he hop?

Yes, he can .

2. Can he whistle?

No, can't.

3. Can she run?

Yes, .

4. Can she hop?

Yes, .

5. Can she whistle?

No, .

6. Can he dance?

No, .

Talk About the Weather!

Listen and say.

How's the weather?

It's **sunny**.

Your Turn

1. sunny

2. rainy

3. cloudy

4. snowy

5. windy

6. stormy

Ss Zz

Listen and say.

sunny

sandwich

sock

zero

zoo

zebra

a b c d e f g h i j k l m n o p q r **s** t u v w x y **z**

Listen and touch.

S   Z

Practice

🎧 Listen and say. Spin and say.

How's the weather?

It's snowy.

Listen and say. Write **s** or **z**.

1. S

2. Z

3. _____

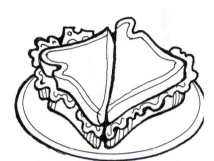

4. _____

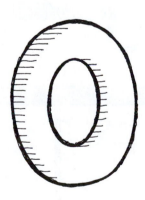

5. _____

6. _____

1. ✓ ○

2. ○ ○

3. ○ ○

4. ○ ○

5. ○ ○

6. ○ ○

7. S Z ○ ○

8. S Z ○ ○

Have Fun!

Climb the mountain.

There's **a flower** on the table.

There are **shoes** on the table, too.

Look! There's a flower on the table, too.

Hmmm.

Your Turn

a pencil case

rulers

an eraser

markers

There are new shoes on the table,
on the table, on the table.
There are new shoes on the table,
on the table, right there.

There's a marker on the table,
on the table, on the table.
There's a marker on the table,
on the table, right there.

 **Learn!**

Listen and say.

Is there a _____ on the desk?
    Yes, there is.
    No, there isn't.

Are there _____ on the desk?
    Yes, there are.
    No, there aren't.

Is there a **pencil case** on the desk?

Yes, there is.

Are there **rulers** on the desk?

No, there aren't.

Your Turn

Is there a ruler on the desk?

1.

2.

3.

Are there pencils on the desk?

4.

5.

6.

Grammar **43**

Practice

🎧 Listen and say. Write.

There are shoes
on the table.

There's a ruler
on the table, too.

🎧 Listen and say. Write.

1. _____ books on the table.

2. _____ a marker on the table, too.

44 ✏️

Practice

Listen and say. Check (✓).

1. Is there a pencil on the table?

- ✓ Yes, there is.
- ☐ No, there isn't.

2. Is there an eraser next to the book?

- ☐ Yes, there is.
- ☐ No, there isn't.

3. Are there markers next to the rulers?

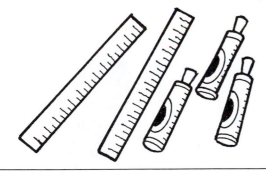

- ☐ Yes, there are.
- ☐ No, there aren't.

4. Are there rulers behind the box?

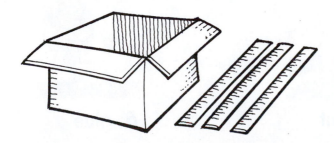

- ☐ Yes, there are.
- ☐ No, there aren't.

45

Talk About Activities!

Listen and say.

I like to cut.

I like to draw.

Your Turn

1. cut

2. draw

3. read

4. sing

5. paint

6. glue

Learn About Sounds!

Listen and say.

lamp leaf lemon

rug rock rope

a b c d e f g h i j k **l** m n o p q **r** s t u v w x y z

Listen and touch.

l r

Practice

🎧 **Listen and match. Write.**

1. I like to cut.

2. I like to draw.

3. I like to paint.

4. I like to sing.

5. I like to glue.

6. I like to read.

Practice

 A. Listen and say. Circle.

1. (l) r

2. l r

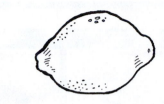

3. l r

4. l r

5. l r

6. l r

B. Listen and say. Write.

1. l

2. r

3. ___

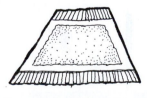

4. ___

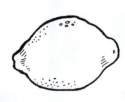

5. ___

6. ___

49

1. ✓ ○

2. ○ ○

3. ○ ○

4. ○ ○

5. ○ ○

6. ○ ○

7. l   r   ○ ○

8. l   r   ○ ○

Have Fun!

Follow the paths.

I like to read.

I like to draw.

Start

Finish

Listen and find.

Your Turn Point and say.

Can he ____?

Is there a ____ on the table?

Role-Play Storytime (Units 3 and 4)

Can you dance?

Look! What are these?

Listen and say.

Your Turn

1	one
2	two
3	three
4	four
5	five
6	six
7	seven
8	eight
9	nine
10	ten
11	eleven
12	twelve
13	thirteen
14	fourteen
15	fifteen
16	sixteen
17	seventeen
18	eighteen
19	nineteen
20	twenty

Shoes for sale!
How much are these?
They're ten dollars.
Ten dollars? Wonderful!
Thank you.
You're welcome!

Shoes for sale!
How much are those?
They're fifteen dollars.
Fifteen dollars? Wonderful!
Thank you.
You're welcome!

Learn!

How much is that?
It's ____ dollars.
How much are those?
They're ____ dollars.

Listen and say.

How much is that?

It's **eleven** dollars.

How much are those?

They're **twenty** dollars.

Your Turn

How much is that?

1. $15

2. $18

3. $17

How much are those?

4. $19

5. $13

6. $14

Practice

🎧 **Match and write. Listen and say.**

How much are these?

Shoes for Sale

$12 twelve
$18 eighteen
$16 sixteen
$10 ten

1. They're sixteen dollars _____ .

2. They're _____ dollars .

3. They're _____ dollars .

4. They're _____ dollars .

58 ✏

Practice

🎧 **Listen and say. Write.**

1.  How much is that?

It's
They're

$5   It's five dollars _____ .

2. How much are those?

 $12

_____ twelve dollars.

3. How much are those?

 $15

_____ fifteen dollars.

4. How much is that?

 $14

_____ fourteen dollars.

59

Talk About Toys!

Listen and say.

TOYS

What do you want?

I want a wagon.

Your Turn

1. a wagon

2. a yo-yo

3. a doll

4. a puzzle

5. a ball

6. a jump rope

Listen and say.

wagon

web

window

yo-yo

yellow

yak

a b c d e f g h i j k l m n o p q r s t u v **w** x **y** z

Listen and touch.

w   y

Practice

🎧 **Listen and say. Write.**

1. I want a doll.

2. _____.

3. _____.

4. _____.

What do you want? Write and draw.

_____.

Practice

🎧 **A. Listen and say. Circle w or y.**

1.

	(w)
	y

2.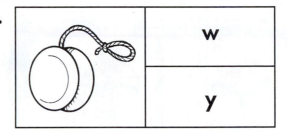

	w
	y

3.

	w
	y

4.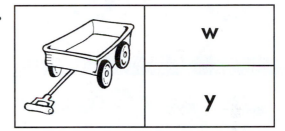

	w
	y

5.

	w
	y

6.

	w
	y

🎧 **B. Listen and say. Circle.**

1. | w |  |

2. | y |  |

🖊 63

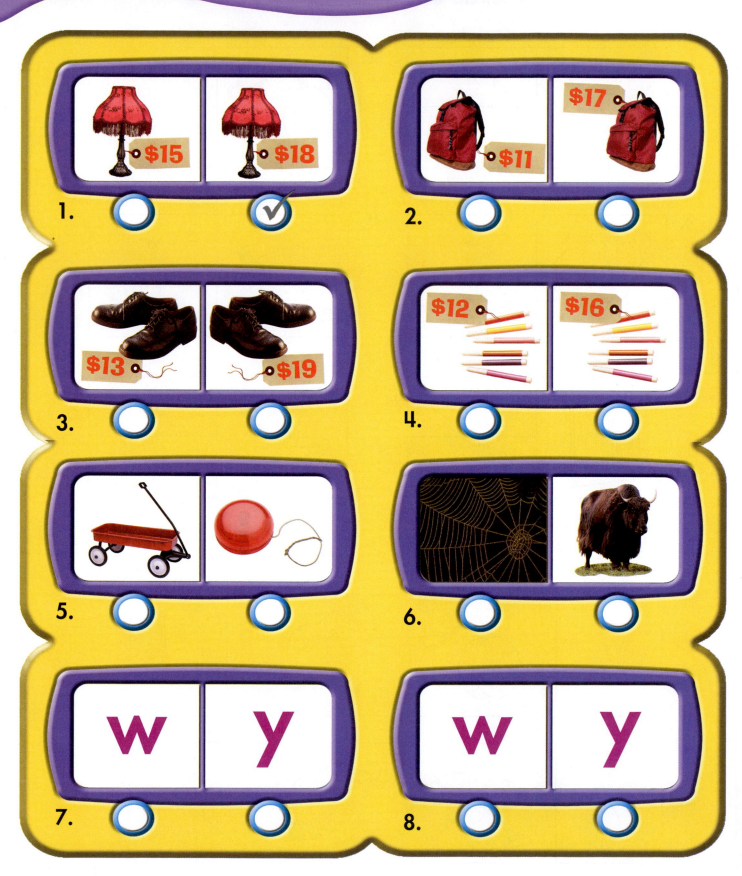

1.

2.

3.

4.

5.

6.

7. w   y

8. w   y

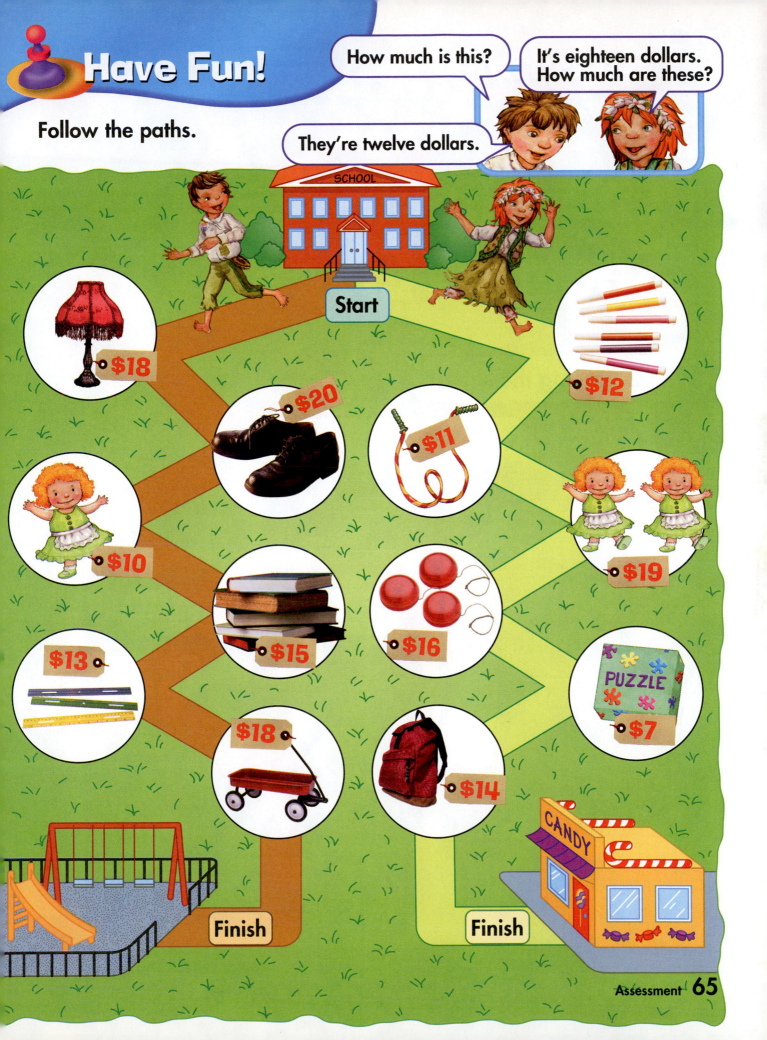

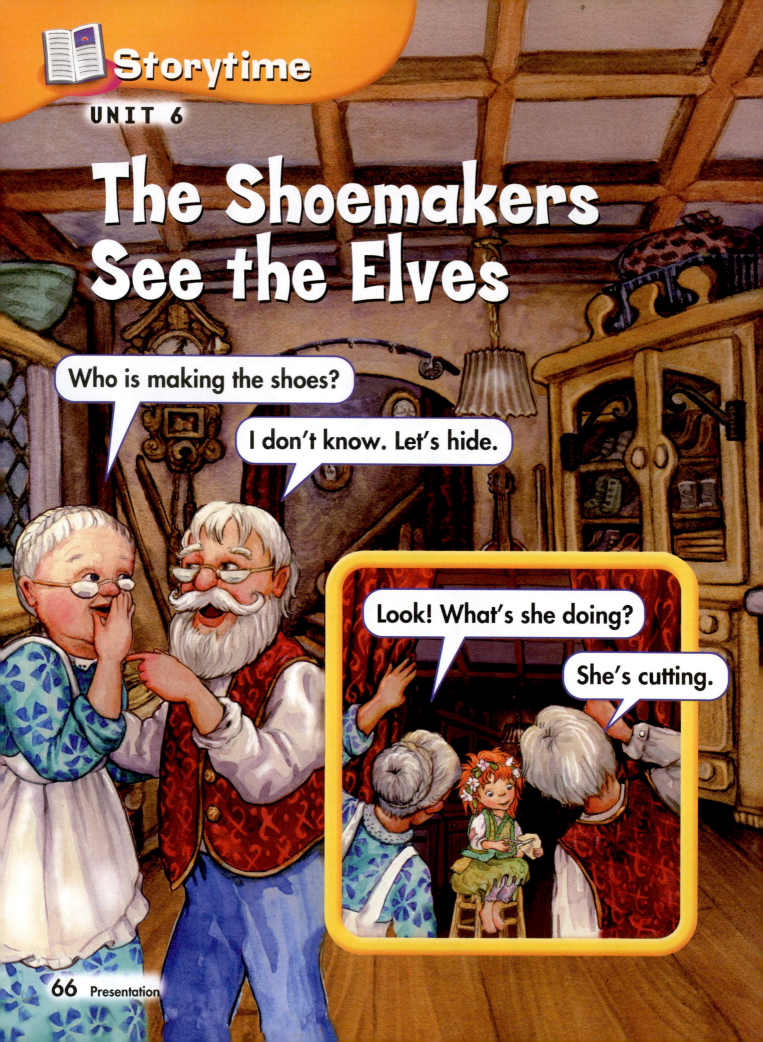

What's he doing?

He's making shoes.

What's **he** doing?

He's making shoes.

Your Turn

He's writing.

She's reading.

He's talking.

She's listening.

What's she doing?
I don't know.
What's she doing?
She's cutting.
Oh. She's cutting.

What's he doing?
I don't know.
What's he doing?
He's writing.
Oh. He's writing.

What are you doing?
I'm ____.

Listen and say.

What are you doing?

I'm **writing**.

Your Turn

1. writing

2. painting

3. thinking

4. jumping

5. walking

6. singing

Practice

🎧 **Listen and say. Write.**

He's She's	reading listening writing talking

1. **What's she doing?**

She's reading   .

2. **What's he doing?**

_____ .

3. **What's she doing?**

_____ .

4. **What's he doing?**

_____ .

5. **What's she doing?**

_____ .

6. **What's he doing?**

_____ .

70 ✏️

 **A. Listen and say. Write.**

 **B. Listen and circle. Write.**

> talking   reading
> writing   listening

1. I'm talking .

2. I'm _____ .

3. I'm _____ .

4. I'm _____ .

Talk About Your Body!

Listen and say.

Touch your **foot**.

Your Turn

1. eye
2. ear
3. nose
4. mouth
5. head
6. hand
7. foot

Listen and say.

hand

hat

head

jam

juice

jacket

a b c d e f g **h** **i** **j** k l m n o p q r s t u v w x y z

Listen and touch.

h   j

🎧 **Listen and write.**

eye   mouth
ear   hand
nose   foot
head

1. eye

2. _____

3. _____

4. _____

5. _____

6. _____

7. _____

Practice

🎧 Listen and say. Match.

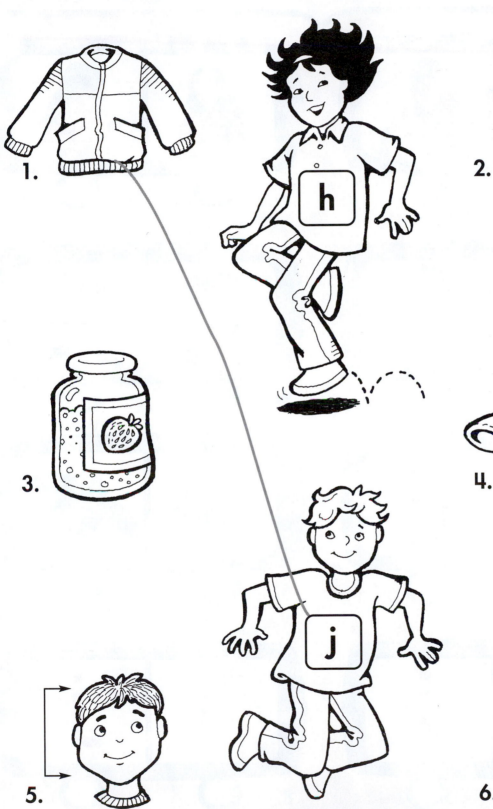

1.

2.

3.

4.

5.

6.

Listen and Choose!

1. ✓
2.
3.
4.
5.
6.

7. **h**   **j**
8. **h**   **j**

Play ball.

What's she doing?

She's reading. What's he doing?

He's singing.

Finish

Start

Start

Finish

Listen and find.

Your Turn   Point and say.

How much is this?

What do you want?

Role-Play Storytime (Units 5 and 6)

How much are these?

Look! What's she doing?

Cuckoo!

It's ten o'clock. Shh! The elves are coming.

Listen and say.

What time is it?

It's **five o'clock.**

Your Turn

 one o'clock

 two o'clock

 three o'clock

 four o'clock

Cuckoo! Cuckoo!
What time is it?
It's one o'clock.
What time is it?
It's one.

Cuckoo! Cuckoo!
What time is it?
It's ten o'clock.
What time is it?
It's ten.

Learn!

Listen and say.

Is he _____?
　Yes, he is.
　No, he isn't.
Is she _____?
　Yes, she is.
　No, she isn't.

Is he talking?

Yes, he is.

Is she writing?

No, she isn't.

Your Turn

Is he talking?

1.

2.

3.

Is she writing?

4.

5.

6.

Grammar **83**

Listen and say. Write the time.

It's	four
	one
	three
	two

What time is it?

1.

It's four o'clock.

2.

_____ o'clock.

3.

_____ o'clock.

4.

_____ o'clock.

🎧 Listen and say. Check (✓).

1. Is he writing?

✓ Yes, he is.

☐ No, he isn't.

2. Is she talking?

☐ Yes, she is.

☐ No, she isn't.

3. Is she reading?

☐ Yes, she is.

☐ No, she isn't.

4. Is he listening?

☐ Yes, he is.

☐ No, he isn't.

5. Is he reading?

☐ Yes, he is.

☐ No, he isn't.

6. Is she singing?

☐ Yes, she is.

☐ No, she isn't.

Talk About a House!

Listen and say.

Where's the kitchen?

Here it is.

Your Turn

1. the kitchen

2. the bedroom

3. the living room

4. the bathroom

5. the workshop

6. the dining room

Learn About Sounds!

Listen and say.

kitchen

kitten

king

queen

quilt

question mark

a b c d e f g h i j **k** l m n o p **q** r s t u v w x y z

Listen and touch.

k qu

Phonics **87**

Practice

🎧 **Listen and find. Write.**

_____
- - - - - - - - - - - -
_____

Where's the bathroom?

bathroom

_____
- - - - - - - - - - - -
_____

_____
- - - - - - - - - - - -
_____

_____
- - - - - - - - - - - -
_____

88 ✏️

Practice

🎧 **A. Listen and say. Write k or qu.**

1. k

2. qu

3. ___

4. ___

5. ___

6. ___

🎧 **B. Listen and say. Match.**

1.

qu

2.

3.

k

4.

5.

6.

89

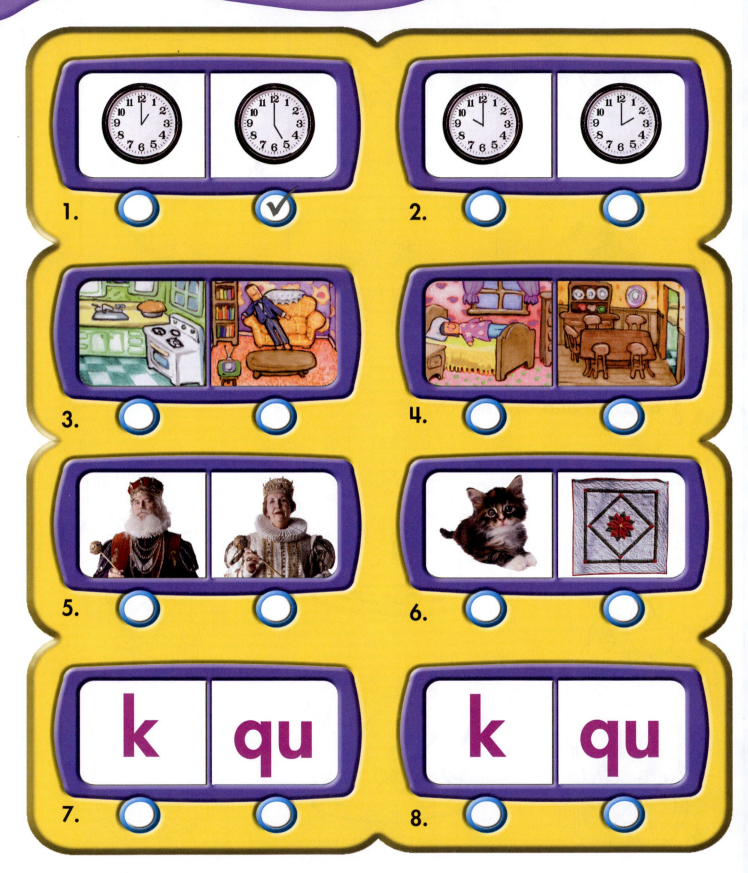

1.

2.

3.

4.

5.

6.

7.

k　qu

8.

k　qu

The Elves Are Happy

What do you have?

I have **a shirt**.

Your Turn

a dress

a skirt

a sweater

a jacket

sneakers

Wow! New clothes!
What do you have?
I have a shirt.
Great!

Wow! New clothes!
What do you have?
I have pants.
Great!

Learn!

Listen and say.

Do you have sneakers?

Yes, I do.

Do you have _____?
Yes, I do.
No, I don't.

don't = do not

Do you have a jacket?

No, I don't.

Your Turn

Do you have _____?

1. a sweater

2. a jacket

3. pants

4. a shirt

5. a dress

6. sneakers

Practice

🎧 Listen and say. Write.

What do you have?

I have a dress.

Write and draw.

I have _____.

I have _____.

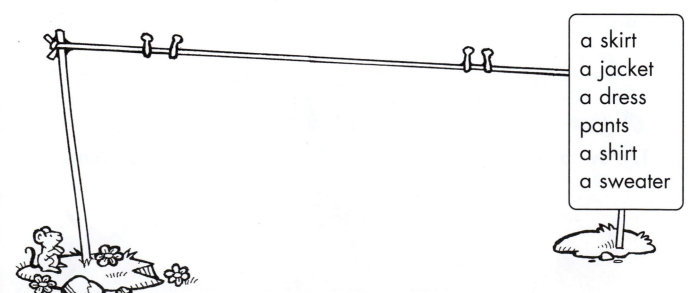

a skirt
a jacket
a dress
pants
a shirt
a sweater

96 ✏️

Practice

🎧 **Listen and say. Write.**

Do you have a skirt?

Yes, I do.

1. Do you have a hat?

No, I don't.

2. Do you have a dress?

Yes, _____.

3. Do you have a sweater?

_____.

Talk About Food!

Listen and say.

Do you want a hot dog?

Yes, please!

No, thank you!

Your Turn

1. a hot dog

2. a hamburger

3. an ice cream cone

4. a sandwich

5. a cookie

6. a box of candy

Listen and say.

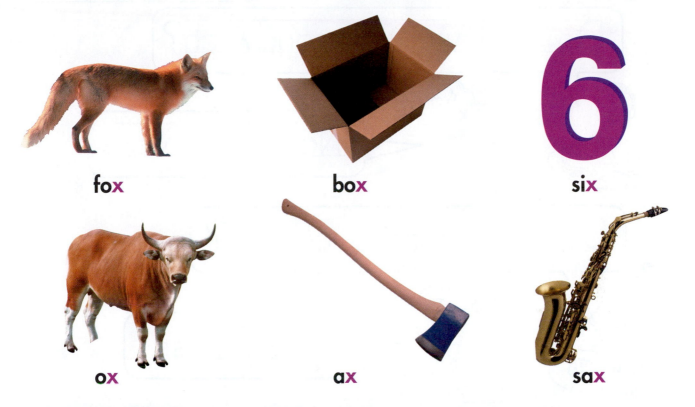

fo**x**   bo**x**   si**x**

o**x**   a**x**   sa**x**

a b c d e f g h i j k l m n o p q r s t u v w **x** y z

Listen and touch.

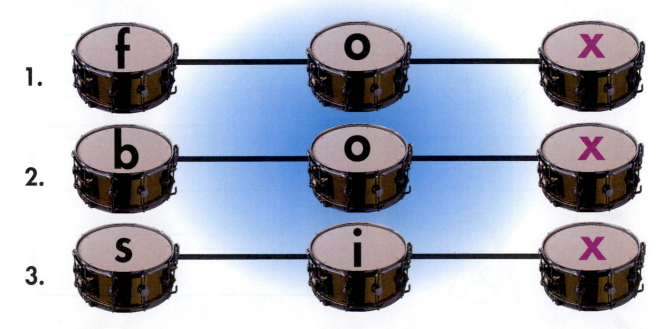

1. f — o — **x**
2. b — o — **x**
3. s — i — **x**

Practice

sandwich	hamburger
cookie	hot dog

1. Do you want a sandwich?

No, thank you.

2. Do you want a cookie?

Yes, please.

3. Do you want a _____?

_____.

4. _____?

_____.

Practice

Listen and say. Circle.

1.

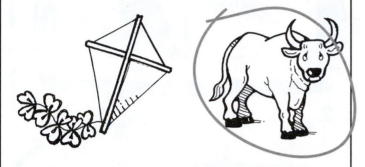

2.

3.

4.

5.

6.

1. ✓

2.

3.

4.

5.

6.

7.

8.

Have Fun!

Look at the clothes!

Listen and find.

Your Turn   Point and say.

Is she singing?

Do you want _____?

Role-Play Storytime (Units 7 and 8)

What time is it?

What do you have?

Word List

A
a	2
an	41
and	28
are	2
aren't	43
at	28
ax	99

B
ball	60
bathroom	86
beautiful	29
bed	20
bedroom	86
behind	15
box	98
busy	15

C
can	28
can't	31
candy	98
chair	20
clothes	80
cloudy	34
coming	81
cookie	98
cup	15
cut	46
cutting	66

D
dance	28
dining room	86
do	60
doctor	3
doing	66
doll	60
dollars	54
door	20
draw	46
dress	93

E
ear	72
eight	55
eighteen	55
eleven	55
elves	66
eraser	41
eye	72

F
fan	21
farmer	3
fast	14
fifteen	54
fish	21
five	55
flower	41
foot	21
for	54
four	55
fourteen	55
fox	99

G
get	15
glue	46
great	54

H
hamburger	98
hammers	8
hand	72
hat	73
have	92
he	2
head	72
help	3
here	86
hop	29
hot dog	98
how much	54
hurry	14

I
I	46
ice cream cone	98
in front of	15
is	2
isn't	43
it's	14

J
jacket	73
jam	73
juice	73
jump rope	60
jump	29
jumping	69

K
king	87
kitchen	86
kitten	87

L
lamp	20
leaf	47
lemon	47
let's	3
listening	67
living room	86
look	2

M
make	3
making	66
map	9
marker	9
mops	8
mouth	72

N
nails	8
nest	9
new	40
next to	15
nine	55
nineteen	55

(no header)
no	31
nose	9
not	2

O
o'clock	80
okay	3
on	14
ox	99

P
paint	46
painting	69
pants	92
pencil case	41
pencils	8
police officer	3
puzzle	60

Q
queen	87
question mark	87
quilt	87

R
rainy	34
read	46
reading	67
ready	2
rock	47
rope	47
rug	47
rulers	8
run	29

S
sale	54
sandwich	35
sax	99
seven	55
seventeen	55
she	2
shirt	92
shoemaker	2
shoes	2
sing	46
singing	69
six	55
sixteen	55
skirt	93
sneakers	93
snowy	34
sock	35
stormy	34
student	3
sunny	34
surprise	93
sweater	93

T
table	14
talking	67
teacher	3
ten	55
thank you	93
that	57

(no header)
the	14
there	40
there's	41
these	40
they	5
they're	5
thinking	69
thirteen	54
those	8
three	55
time	80
to	46
too	2
touch	72
twelve	55
twenty	55
two	55

U
under	15

V
van	21
vest	21
violin	21

W
wagon	60
walk	29
walking	69
want	60
weather	34
web	61
welcome	93
what	8
where's	14
whistle	28
who	2
window	20
windy	34
wonderful	55
work	14
workshop	86
writing	67

Y
yak	61
yellow	61
yes	31
you	28
you're	93
your	72
yo-yo	60

Z
zebra	35
zero	35
zoo	35

Classroom English

Sit down.

Stand up.

Open your book.

Close your book.

Raise your hand.

Clap your hands.

Pick up your book.

Put down your book.

Listen.

Look at the board.

Write.

Come here.

Picture Dictionary

ball		cup	
bathroom		cut	
bed		dance	
bedroom		dining room	
candy		doctor	
chair		doll	
cloudy		door	
cookie		draw	

dress		hamburger	
ear		hammer	
eraser		hand	
eye		hat	
farmer		head	
flower		hop	
foot		hot dog	
glue		ice cream cone	

jacket	mop
jump	mouth
jump rope	nail
kitchen	nose
lamp	paint
listen	pants
living room	pencil
marker	pencil case

police officer		shirt	
puzzle		shoes	
rainy		shoemaker	
read		sing	
rug		skirt	
ruler		sneakers	
run		snowy	
sandwich		stormy	

student		walk	
sunny		whistle	
sweater		window	
table		windy	
teacher		workshop	
think		write	
wagon		yo-yo	

16

The Elves and the Shoemaker

1

12

5

2

15

6

11

14

3

10

7

4

13

8

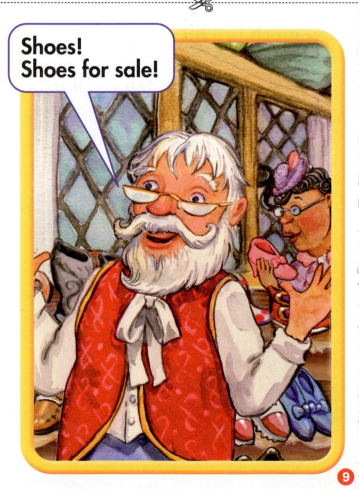

9